# HOUETTES

## A Pictorial Archive of Varied Illustrations

Edited by
Carol Belanger Grafton

DOVER PUBLICATIONS, INC.
NEW YORK

Published in Canada by General Publishing Company, Ltd., 30 Lesmill Road, Don Mills, Toronto, Ontario.
Published in the United Kingdom by Constable and Company, Ltd., 10 Orange Street, London WC2H 7EG.

*Silhouettes: A Pictorial Archive of Varied Illustrations* is a new work, first published by Dover Publications, Inc., in 1979.

DOVER *Pictorial Archive* SERIES

*International Standard Book Number: 0-486-23781-8*
*Library of Congress Catalog Card Number: 78-75362*

Manufactured in the United States of America
Dover Publications, Inc.
31 East 2nd Street
Mineola, N.Y. 11501

# Publisher's Note

A silhouette is a portrait or scene depicted in an outline that has been filled in solid. It is an ancient art form, examples of which can be found in Paleolithic cave paintings. The Greeks are known to have made silhouettes by tracing shadows cast by the sun. In the East, as early as the Tang dynasty (618–907), the Chinese were executing cut-paper designs that are close in feeling to silhouettes. Later examples can be found in Bernd Melchers' *Traditional Chinese Cut-Paper Designs* (Dover 23581-5) and Theodore Menten's *Chinese Cut-Paper Designs* (Dover 23198-4). India developed a shadow theater that later spread to the Middle East and Europe. Egyptian shadow puppets of mounted Mameluke heroes have survived from the eleventh century. In the nineteenth century, Le Chat Noir, a Parisian café, featured elaborate shadow plays, some of them designed by the artist Caran d'Ache. Shadow plays are still seen occasionally as a novelty on television, and survive, in more traditional form, in places such as Indonesia.

In the West, the silhouette enjoyed its greatest popularity from the mid-eighteenth to the mid-nineteenth centuries. It was an inexpensive means of portraiture and also possessed a unique charm, capturing the essence of a personality with a minimum of detail and calling on the viewer to use his own imagination. In England, such works were generally known as "shades" or "shadow portraits" well into the nineteenth century. The name by which they are now known is derived from Etienne de Silhouette (1709–67), the controller-general of France. Infamous for his tight financial policies, he amused himself by cutting portraits from paper. Thus, in its strictest sense, a silhouette is cut, either freehand, using the eye alone as a guide, or by following lines that have either been traced by the artist or drawn mechanically. Various means were developed to aid the artist in getting an accurate likeness cast on paper: the camera obscura, chairs with clamps for holding the subject steady, devices to prevent candles from wavering, machines that cut automatically as a tracer was passed over the subject's profile. One device, the Prosopographus, used an automaton to trace the profile. Although Goethe (who was fond of cutting profiles) held that only life-sized silhouettes were worthy of consideration, means such as the pantograph (which had been developed in 1631) were available to make accurate reductions that could be used on jewelry, snuffboxes, lockets, etc. Some silhouettes were cut in reverse, i.e., white paper had a profile cut from it, the inner portion of which was discarded and the outer, negative, portion of which was mounted on black paper.

Silhouettes were also painted, again either freehand or using some mechanical aids. Most frequently they were done on plaster, glass or enamel. When executed on convex glass, the work was often backed by a colored medium such as wax.

Every art form has its own masters, and several artists became famous for their silhouettes. John Miers' (1756–1821) portraits on plaster have an uncommon delicacy. The cut-paper portraits of August Edouart (1769–1861) dazzle us with their technical virtuosity. The famous English illustrator Arthur Rackham (1867–1939) executed two books, *Cinderella* and *Sleeping Beauty*, entirely in crisp, witty silhouettes. The silhouette is infinitely adaptable and, as this collection shows, can accommodate any style, ranging from rococo elegance to flowing art-nouveau curves. A selection of a later style is available in Jo Anne C. Day's *Decorative Silhouettes of the Twenties* (Dover 23152-6).

The present collection has been taken from many sources as a practical aid for artists and designers. It is not intended to be a definitive or systematic study of the silhouette, although it is probably as thorough a compilation as is generally available today. Looking through it, the reader must be struck by the multiplicity of uses to which the silhouettes can be put—spot illustrations, decoupage, cameo-like jewelry ornamentation, etc. The examples included demonstrate the versatility of the silhouette. Equally convincing are the depictions of the Passion of Christ and the several tranquil eighteenth-century domestic scenes. The material has been organized into the following categories: men's profiles (pp. 1–5); men in full figure (pp. 6–37); women's profiles (pp. 38–41); women in full figure (pp. 42–58); children (pp. 59–74); groups and scenes (pp. 75–107); an alphabet in silhouette (pp. 108 and 109); birds and animals (pp. 110–127); other subjects from nature (pp. 128–135); ships (pp. 136 and 137).

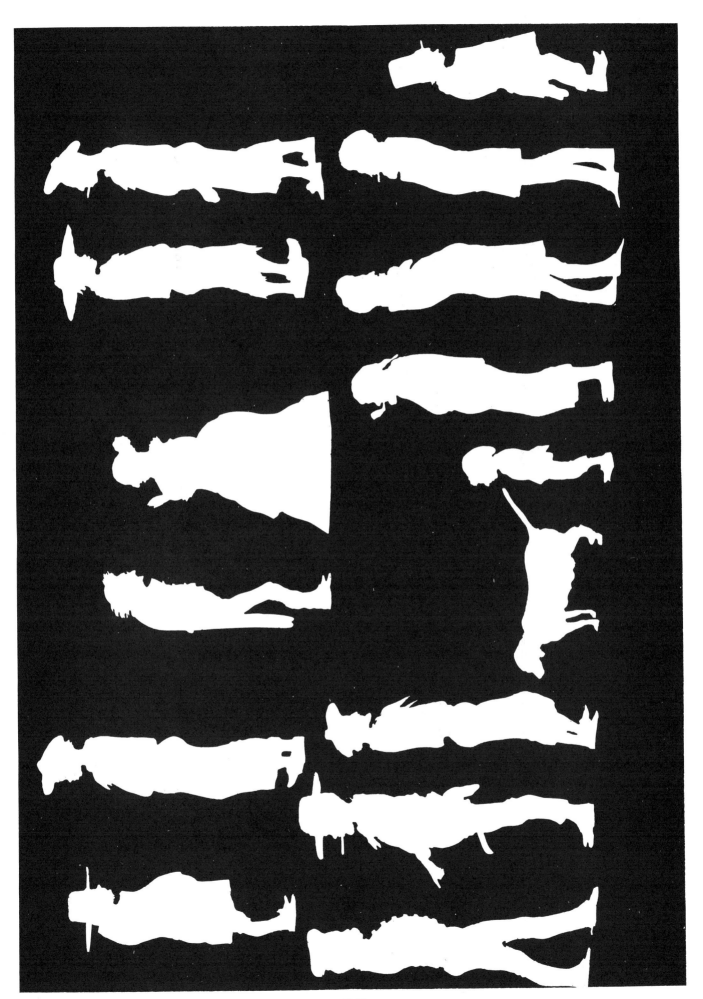

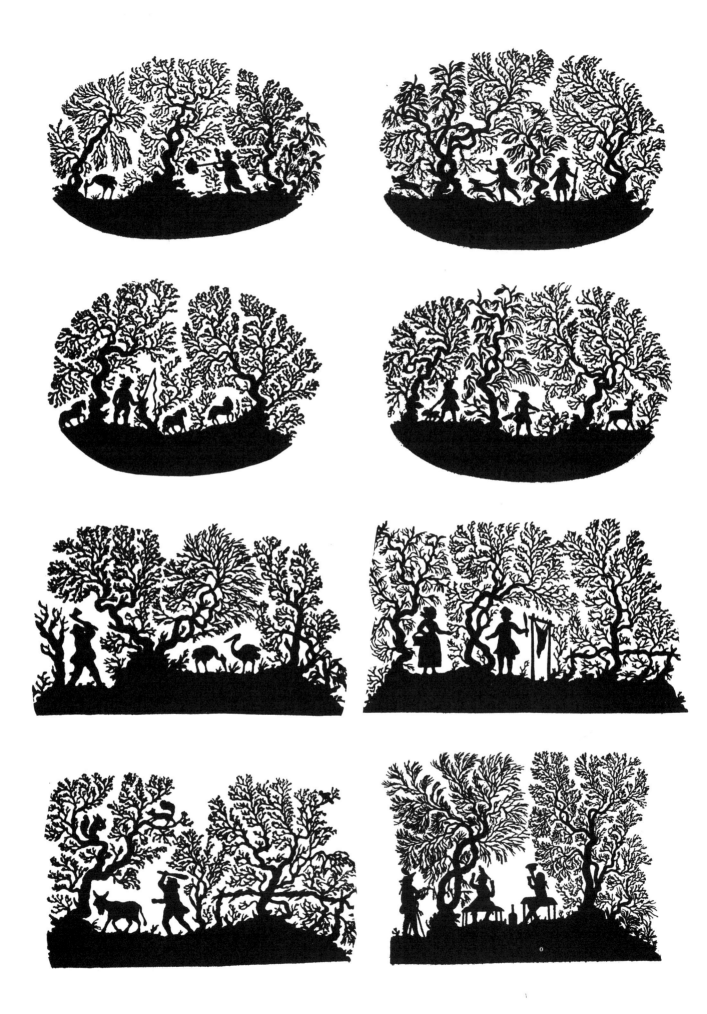